Snail Tr

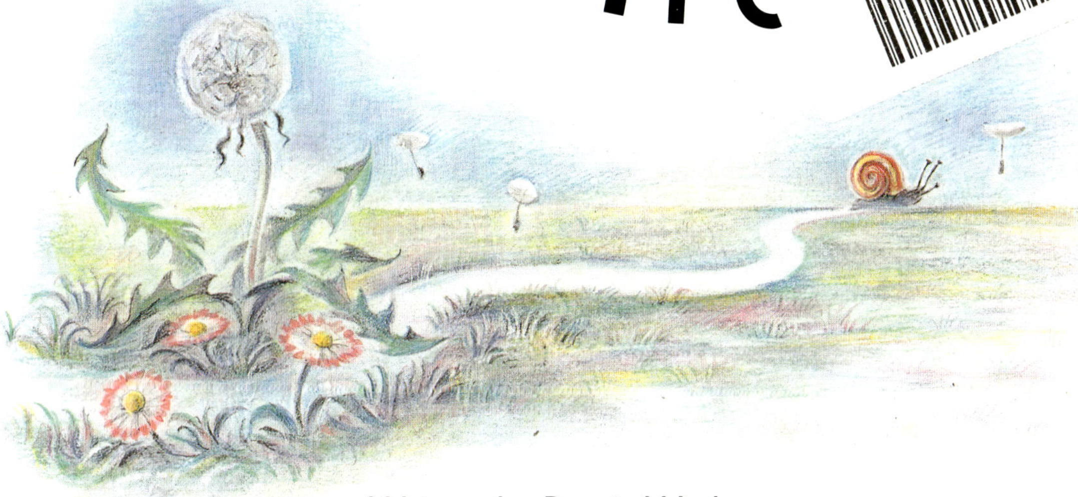

Written by Barrie Wade
Illustrated by Tony Escott

Collins *Educational*
An imprint of HarperCollins*Publishers*

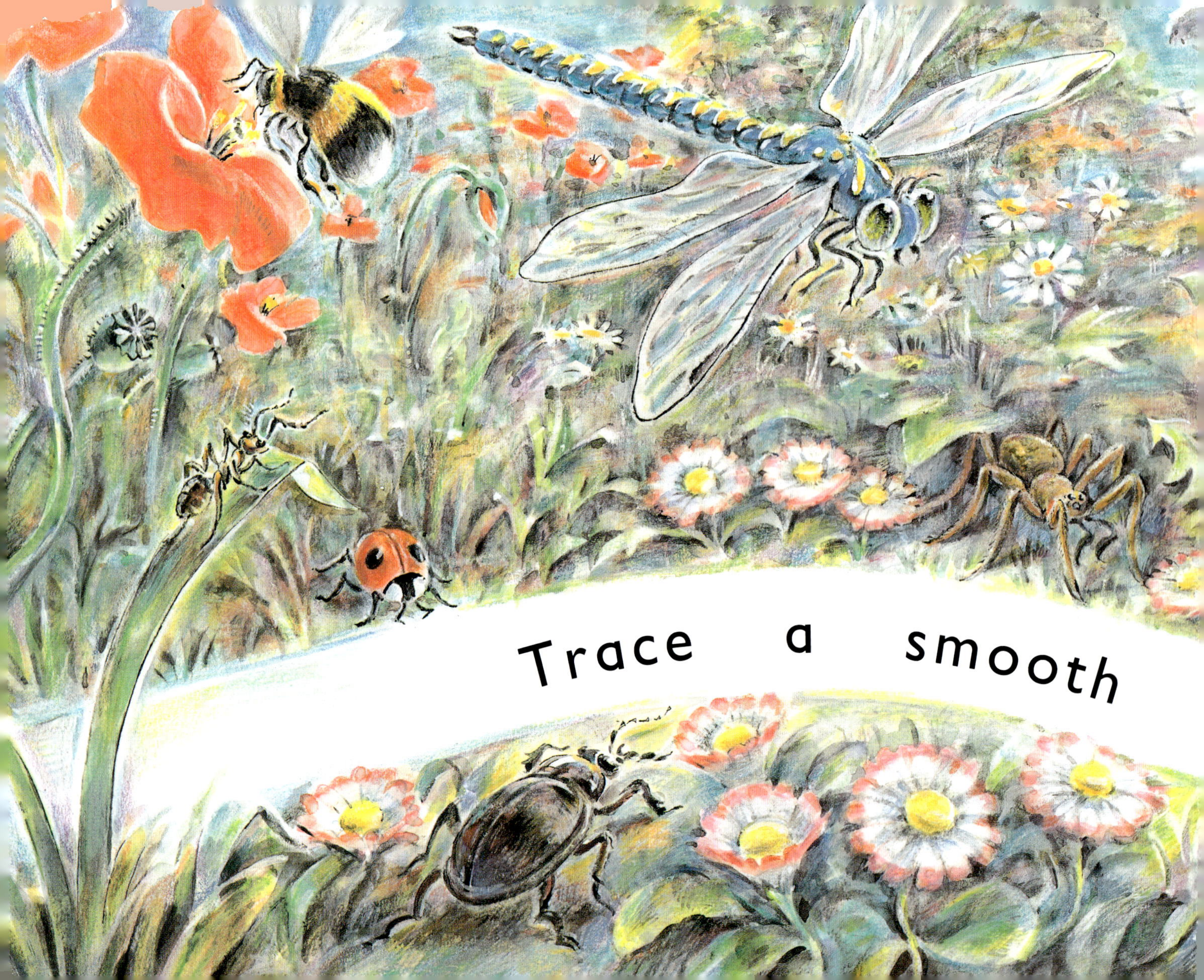

Trace a smooth

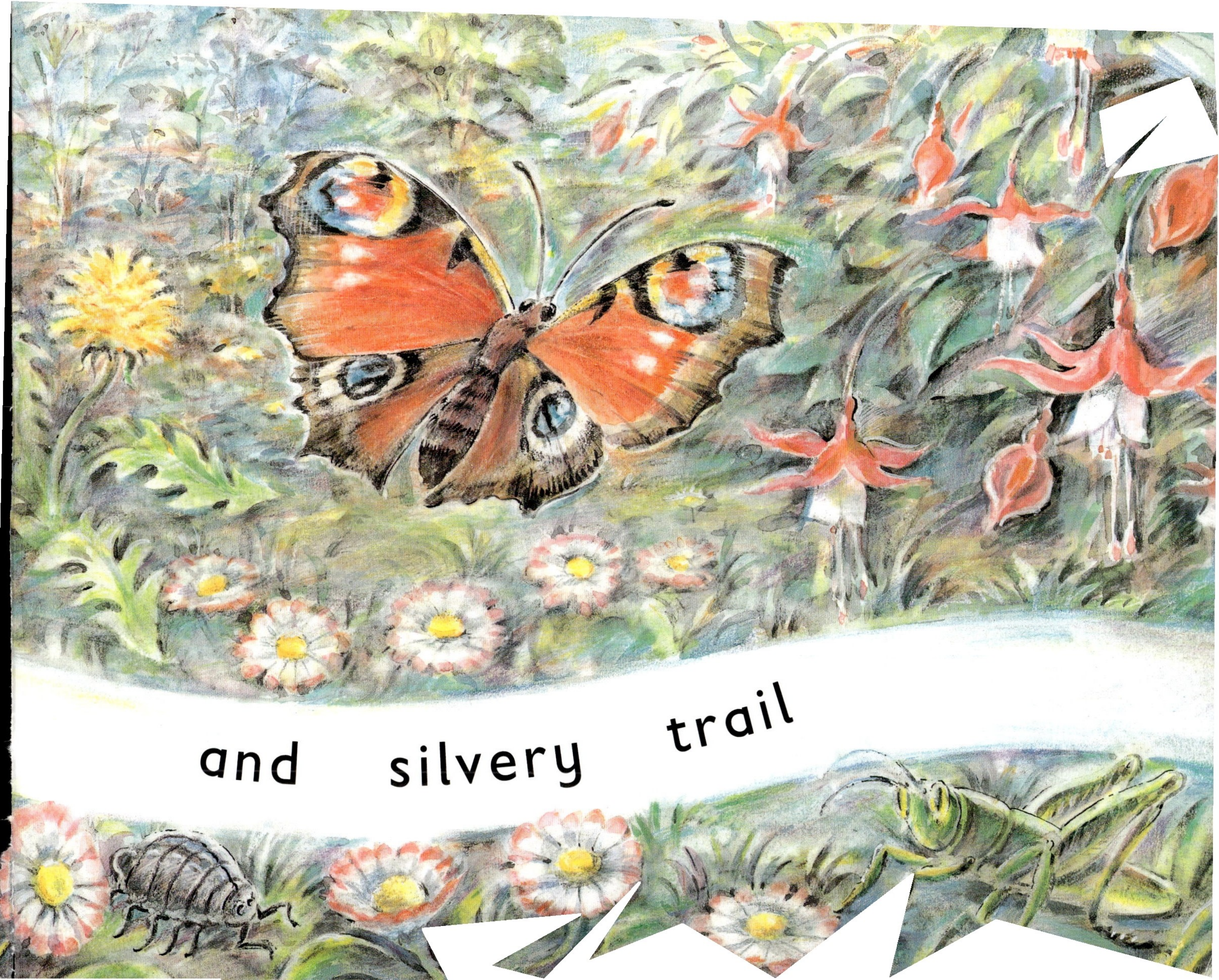

and silvery trail

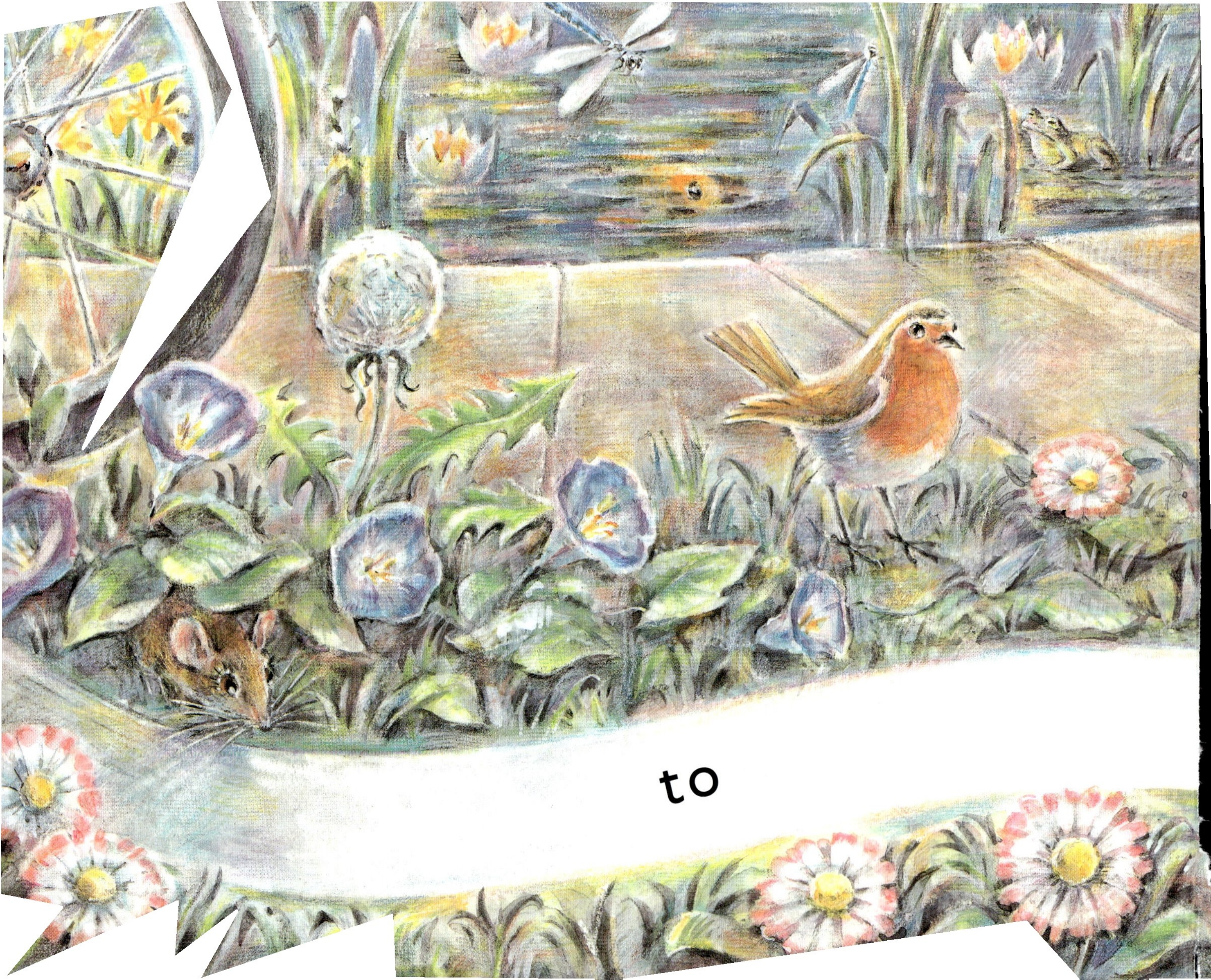
to

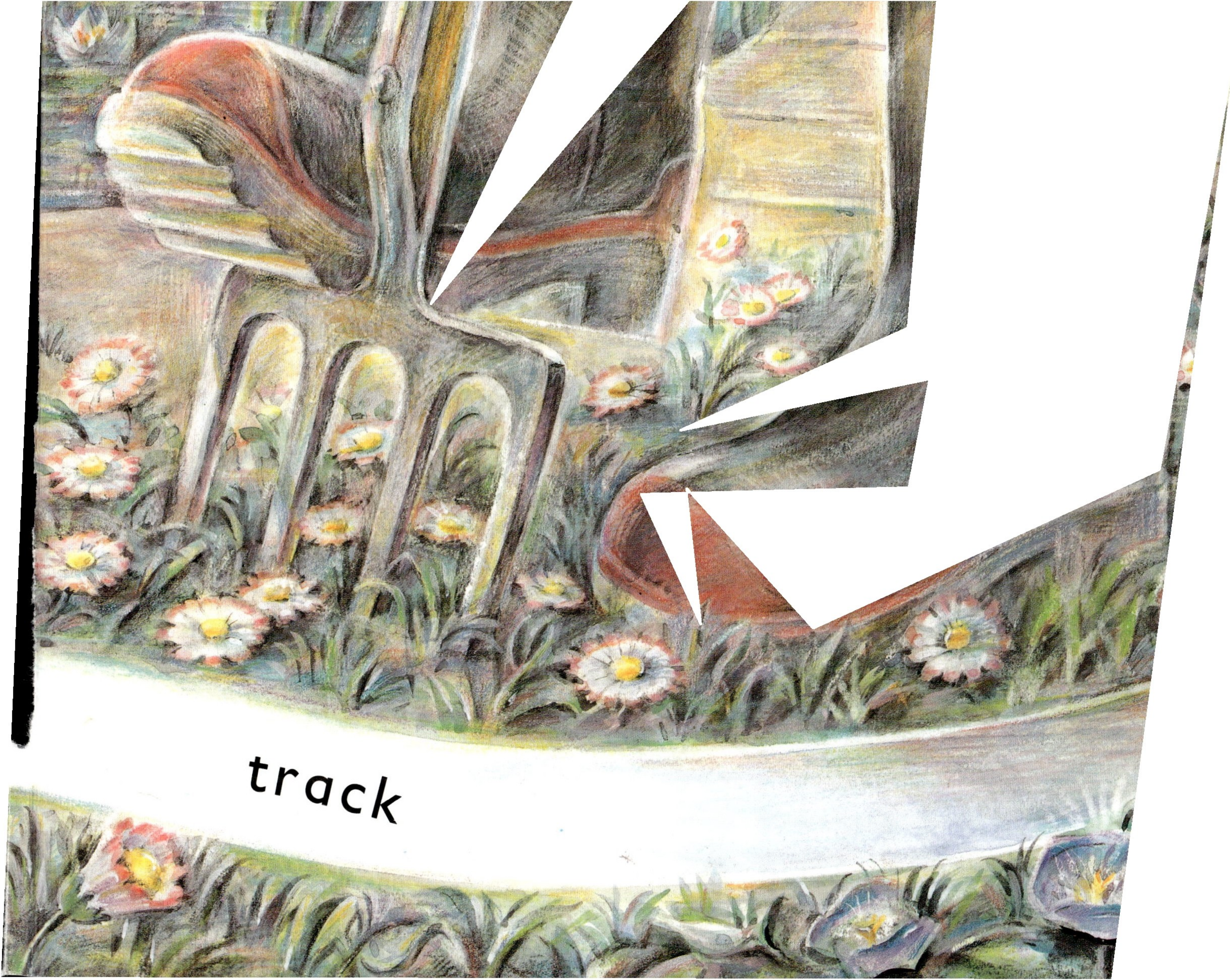
track

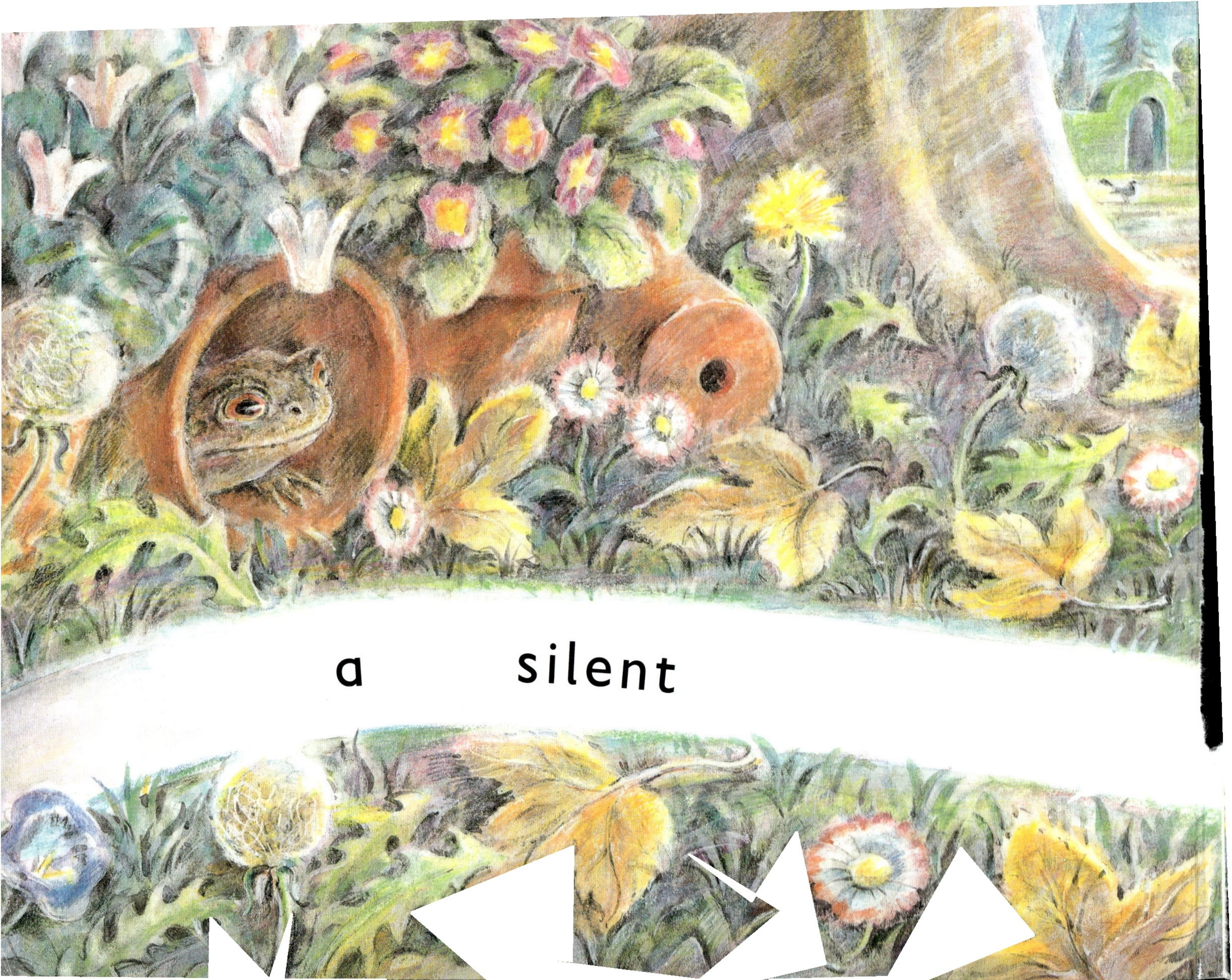

a silent

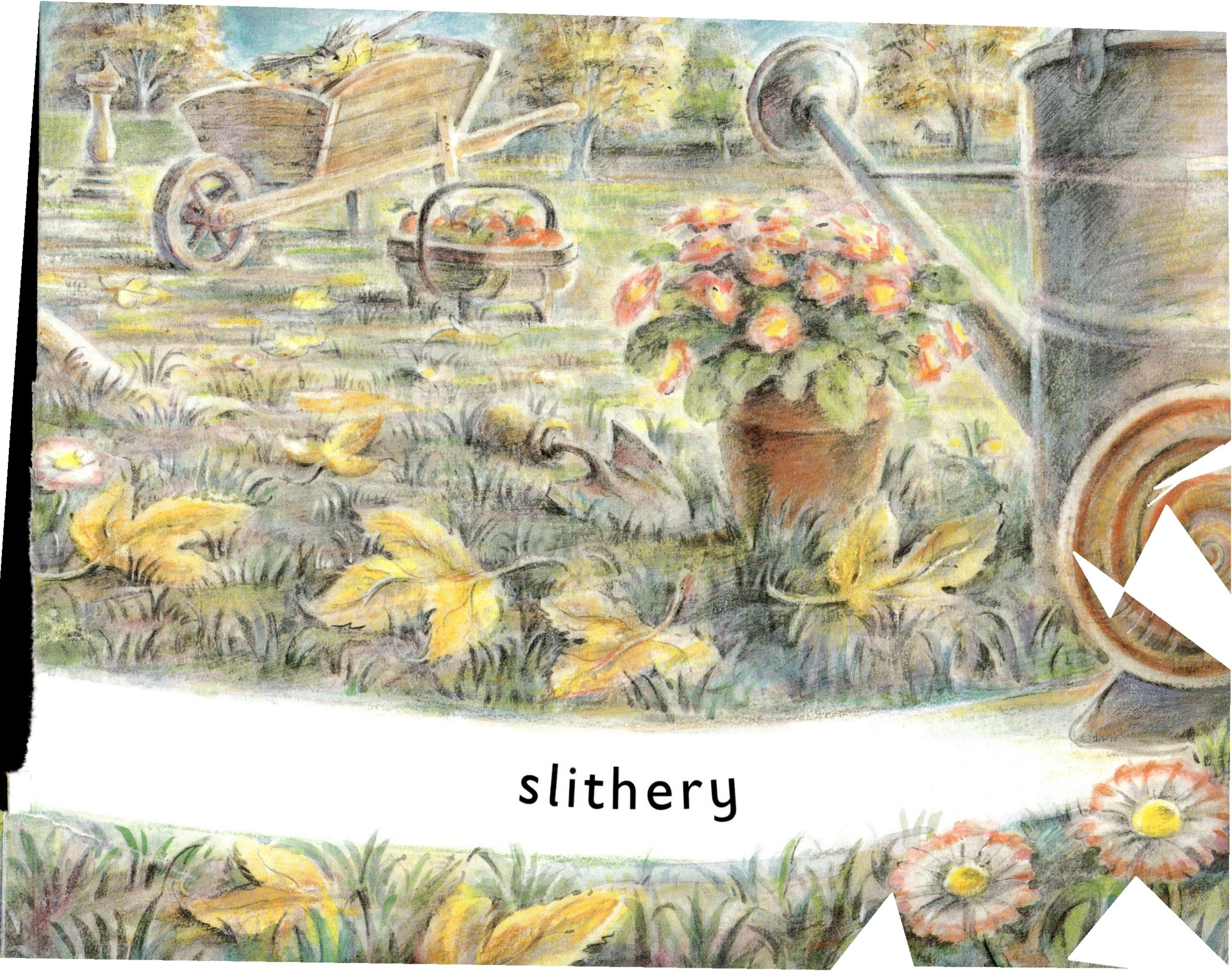

slithery

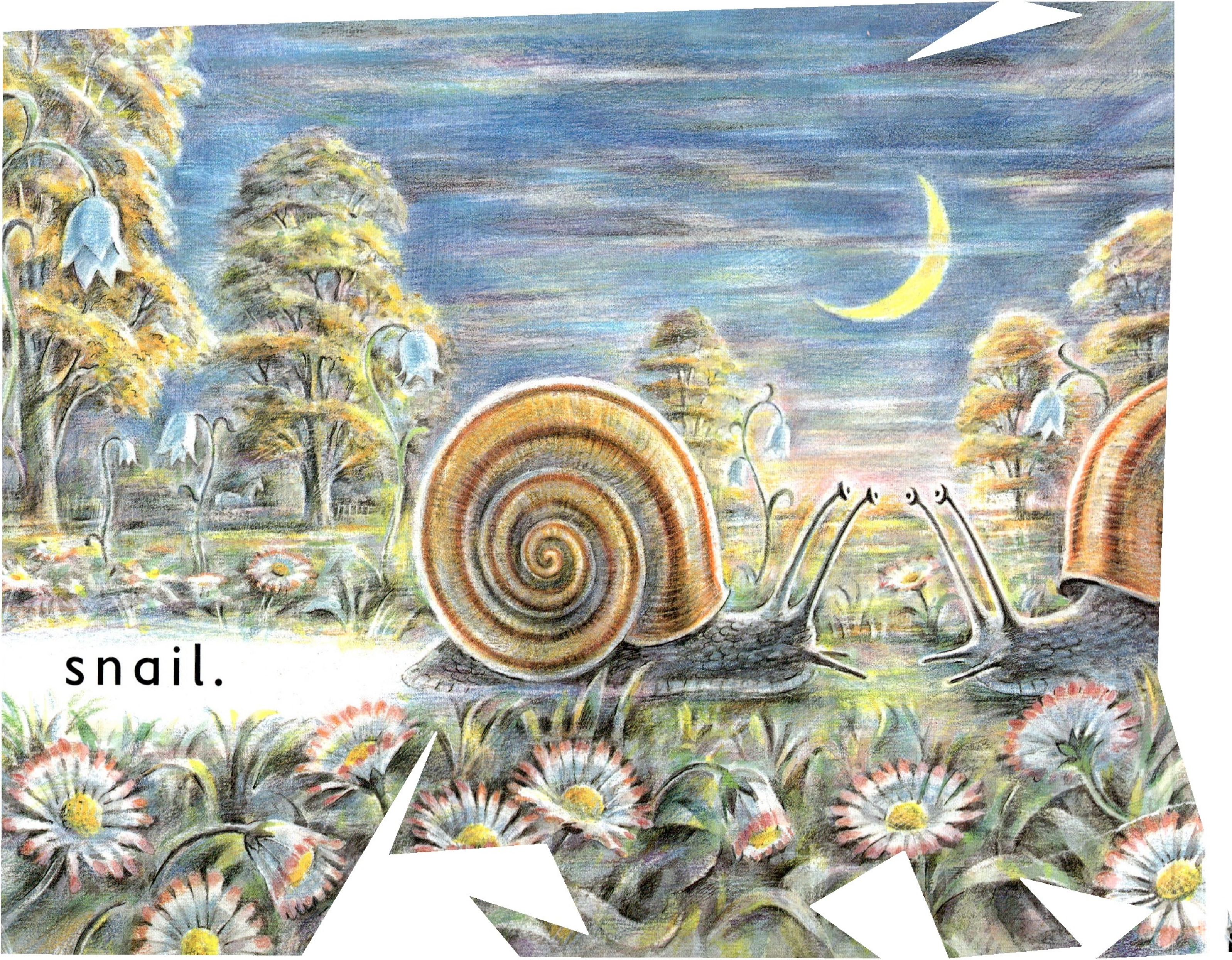

snail.